Geography CE/KS3
Topic Booklet

Settlement

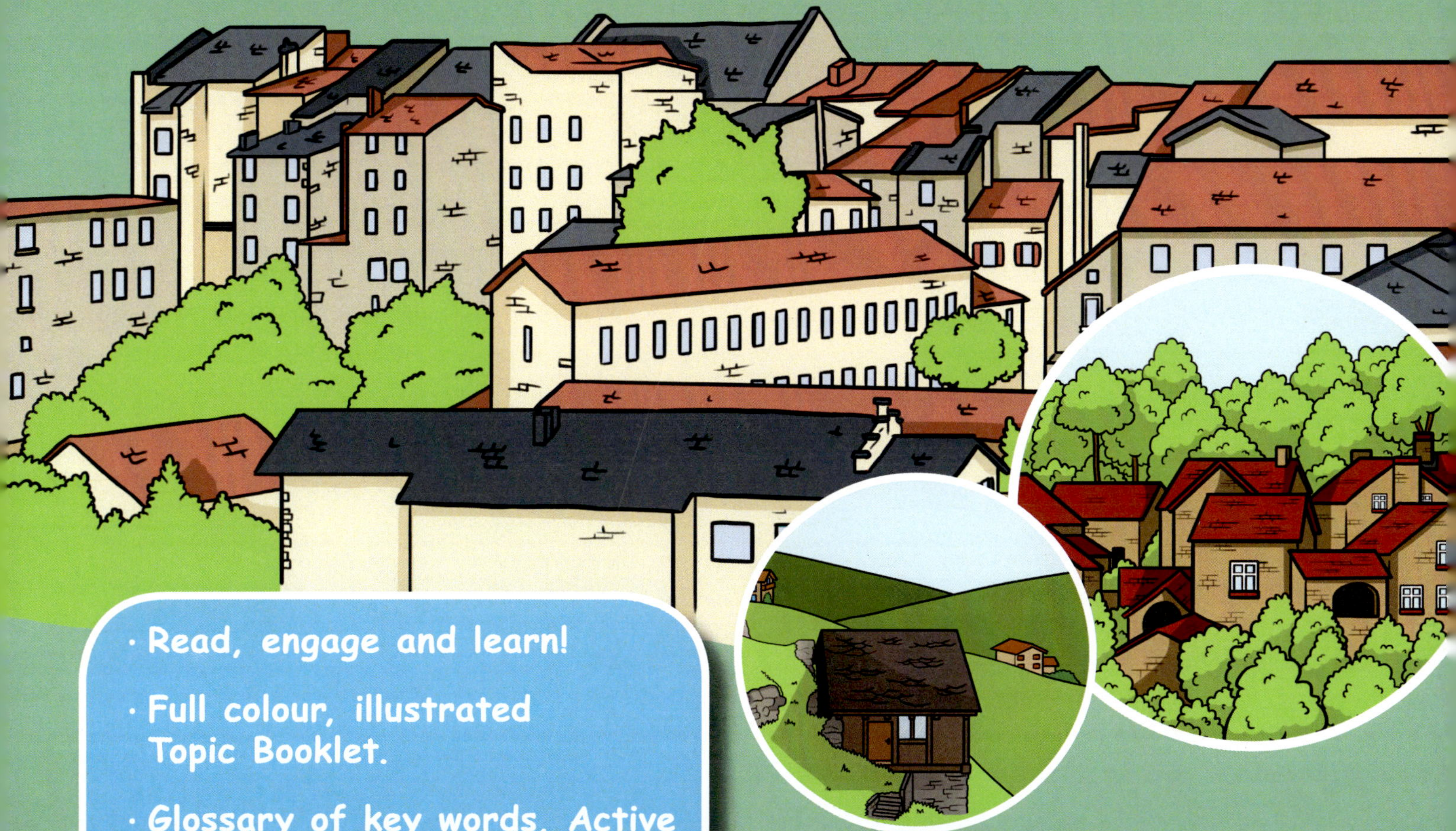

- Read, engage and learn!
- Full colour, illustrated Topic Booklet.
- Glossary of key words, Active Learning Game & Flashcards.
- Ideal for ISEB 13+ Common Entrance and KS3 pupils.

Endorsed by:
ISEB Independent Schools Examinations Board

This Oaka™ Books Topic Booklet goes hand in hand with the Active Learning Pack on this topic. The pack includes a Write Your Own Notes Booklet, an Active Learning Game and Question & Answer Flashcards.

Fresh Focus on Learning

Oaka™ BOOKS

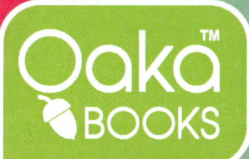

Settlement Glossary

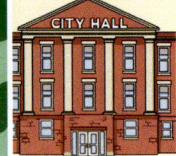
Administrative (ad-mini-strah-tiv): local government offices.

Brownfield Site: disused or derelict urban land that can be redeveloped.

Central Business District: this is the most accessible part of the town or city and is where most business is located.

Commercial: shops or shopping malls in large towns and cities.

Green Field Site: areas of land that are being built on. Encourages urban sprawl.

Green Belts: restricts building in open areas, to control urban sprawl.

Industrial: factories that make products are usually placed in settlements, for people to work in.

Megacity: cities with a 10 million+ population.

Population: the number of people living in a place.

Residential: housing within settlements for people to live in.

Rural: the countryside.

Services: these include doctors' surgeries, schools and hospitals.

Settlement: a place where people live.

Site: the exact location of a settlement.

Situation: the location of a settlement in comparison to its surroundings.

Tourism: people travelling to see attractions in a particular location.

Urban: a town or a city.

Urban Sprawl: the spreading of a city into rural areas.

What is a Settlement?

1 What is a Settlement?

- A **settlement** is where people live.
- It is **any form of dwelling**: from 1 small house to a megacity (millions of people in a city).

2 Settlement Sizes

- Settlements can **vary in size**, from very small to very large!
- They can be **permanent** (fixed) or **temporary** (only there for a short time).

3 Site

- Where settlements start, it is called a **site**.
- In **earlier times**, different sites were **chosen** for **different reasons**.

- These reasons included...

4 1. Flat, Dry Land

- This makes building easier and safer, and does not flood.

Site Factors

5 ## 2. Local Materials

- To build homes with and to use as fuel (such as wood and stone).

6 ## 3. Water Supply

- Used for drinking, transport, washing, cooking, etc.

7 ## 4. Good Farm Land

- To grow food on.

8 ## 5. Shelter

- To protect from bad weather (such as near a forest).

Site Factors

9   6. Defence

- To protect from attackers (such as near a hill top or a river bend).

10   7. Transport

- Bridging points where transport routes (over land and water) converge assisting trade and commerce.

11   Situation

- **Situation** is where the settlement is **in relation to other settlements** and **features**.
- Is it near a forest? Or maybe a larger town.

12   Growing Cities

- If a settlement had **lots of good site factors** and a **good situation**, then it could **grow**!
- Many big cities in the UK have grown because they have good site factors and situation.

Types of Settlements

13 Hierarchy

- Settlements can be **ranked in order.**
- This is called a **hierarchy.**
- Order is decided by **size, population** and **services** (range and number).

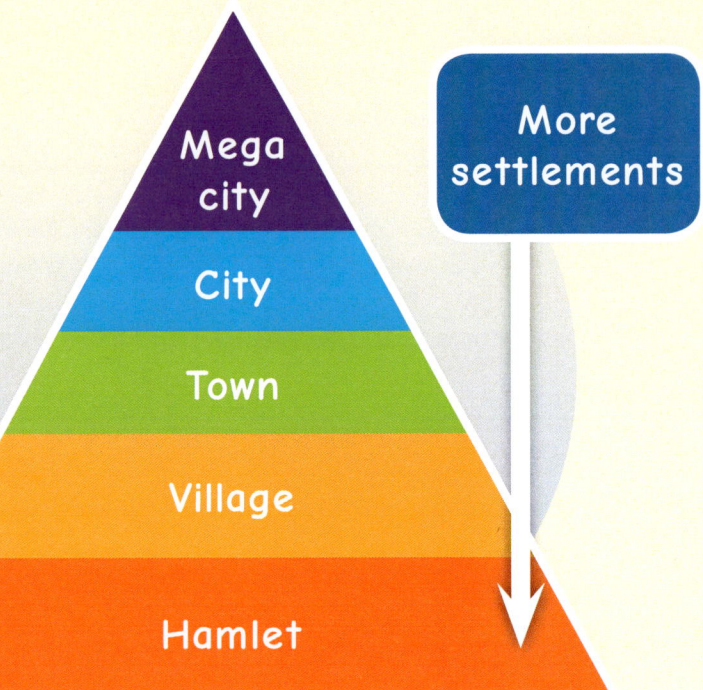

Mega city

City

Town

Village

Hamlet

More settlements

Fewer but more important and bigger

14 Hamlet

- **A hamlet** has **less than 100 people** dwelling there.
- It has a **very small** group of homes.
- It has **few**, or **no shops** or **facilities**.
- They do not have a church.

15 Village

- **Villages** have 100 to 1,000 people.
- They have **more functions**, such as a church, a shop and a post-office.
- They may even have a primary school, a doctor's practice and a pub.

Types of Settlements

16   Town

- **Towns** have a **population** of 1,000 to 100,000 people.
- They have a range of functions.

- These include many **shops**, **schools**, **train stations**, a **bank**, **dentist** and a small **hospital**.

17   City

- **Cities** have more than 100,000 people living there.
- They have a very wide range of functions as well as **specialised functions**.

- These include a **university**, **sports stadiums**, **large hospitals**, **large shopping centres**, a **cathedral** and **museums**.

Did you know?
In the past, a city always had a cathedral or a university.
Now the Queen decides which places are cities!

Types of Settlements

18 — Megacity

- A megacity has **more than 10 million people** living there.
- It has the **same functions** as a **city**, but it's **much bigger!**

19 — Remember!

- What may be a village in one part of the world, could be thought of as a town in another!

Town   Village

20 — Is it a city, a town or a village?

- It is not easy as you think! **Three things** need to be thought about:

Number and range of services (and how far people may travel to use the services).

Distance between the settlement and others (many hamlets may be close together, but towns will have a bigger distance between them).

Groceries   BANK   Post Office   Pharmacy

Population Size

Settlement Patterns

21 Linear

- Settlements develop in a pattern.

Linear (in a line):
- along a **road**, **valley** or **coastline**.
- often on a **main road** between two settlements.

22 Dispersed

Dispersed (spread out):
- **isolated**.
- farms and houses usually in areas with **steep relief.**

23 Nucleated

Nucleated (from the word nucleus, a core or central point):
- often centred around a **water supply/river source**, or at a **crossroad.**
- also may have been built around a **castle** or **market place.**

Settlement Patterns

24   Planned

Planned:

- Towns which are planned on a **square** or **grid pattern**.
- These tend to be **new** settlements.

25   Urban Sprawl

- As **transport improved** in the **1920s**, people could live further from work.
- **Urban sprawl** developed and **more linear settlements** grew along new **transport links**.

Central Business District

Housing

26   Green Belts

- **Green Belts** were begun to **control** urban sprawl.
- They **restrict** building in rural areas, where it is very difficult to get planning permission.

Green Belt

27   Settlement Functions

The functions of a settlement are its **purposes**.

The functions can be split into **6 main groups**:

- Commercial
- Residential
- Administrative
- Services
- Industrial
- Tourism

A settlement may start with one function, but some may be added.

Settlement Functions

28 Commercial

- This includes shops in small villages, to large shopping centres in towns and cities.
- These shopping centres may also include sports and cinemas.

29 Residential

- **All settlements** have housing **(residential function)**.
- But some are built to **provide extra housing** because a city may be **overcrowded**.

- These can be called **dormitory settlements** and the people **commute** to work.

30 Residential

- Dormitory settlements are found **outside** the main settlement.
- This consists of **terraced**, **semi-detached** and **detached housing** for people to live in.

- There are also **retirement villages** which offer **extra support** for older people.

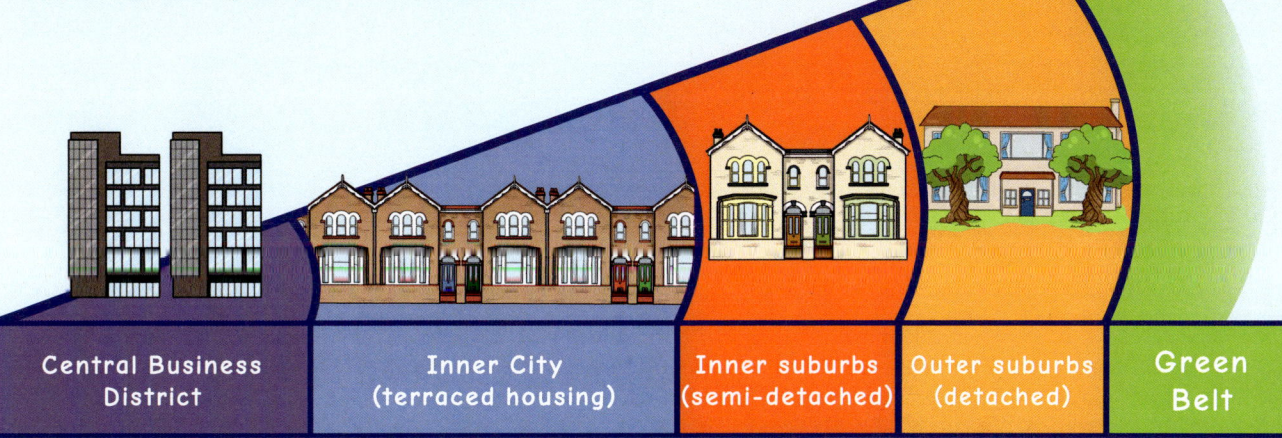

Central Business District | Inner City (terraced housing) | Inner suburbs (semi-detached) | Outer suburbs (detached) | Green Belt

Settlement Functions

31 Administrative

- Local government has offices and runs public services.
- These are usually found in larger settlements.

32 Services

- As the size of a settlement increases, so does the range and number of services.
- These include **doctors' surgeries**, **schools** and **hospitals**.

33 Industrial

- **Companies** which **manufacture** (make) products, put their factories in a settlement.
- **Big cities** often have **many industries** because they need **people to work** in the factory.
- Some industries may **locate** near **smaller settlements**.
- This is because the **price of land** may be **lower**.

Settlement Functions

34   Tourism

- Many settlements have a **tourist function**.
- **Big cities** have many **attractions**, such as **museums**, **art galleries** and **theatres**.

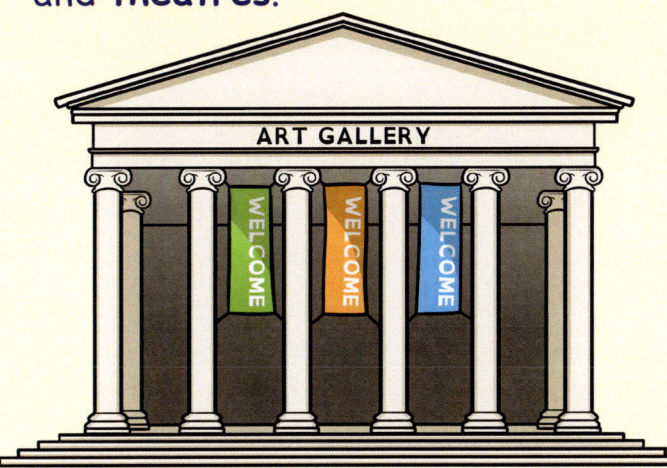

35   Tourism

- Many **small villages** are **pretty** and **quiet**.
- **Seaside towns** attract many people for day trips and holidays.

Why do some settlements grow and others don't?

36 Suburbanisation

- Villages or small towns which are near a city, may **grow bigger**.
- This is because people can **commute** (called **suburbanisation**, pronounced sub-erb-an-i-zay-shon).

37 Rural Villages

- Many **rural villages** lose young people, because there are **no jobs**.
- New industries creates jobs and people move to that area.

I'm moving away from this village to a new area with jobs!

38 Flat Land

- Places that are **accessible** (easy to get to) and have **flat land**, means that people will **build** there.

This place is perfect to build on!

39 Settlements Not Growing

- If there is **no competition** from other settlements or few site advantages, a settlement may **not** grow.

Shops and Services

40 — The Threshold

- The smallest number of people needed to support shops and services is called the **threshold**.

- For example, a village probably needs 300 people who live in or near it, to have one shop. This is a threshold of 300.

- A large store, such as Marks and Spencer, needs a bigger town with a **large threshold** to support it (probably 100,000 people!).

Small threshold

VILLAGE SHOP

M&S

Large threshold

41 — The Catchment Area

- Shops also have a **range**: it depends on the distance people will **travel** to reach it.

- The **catchment area** is where the customers live.

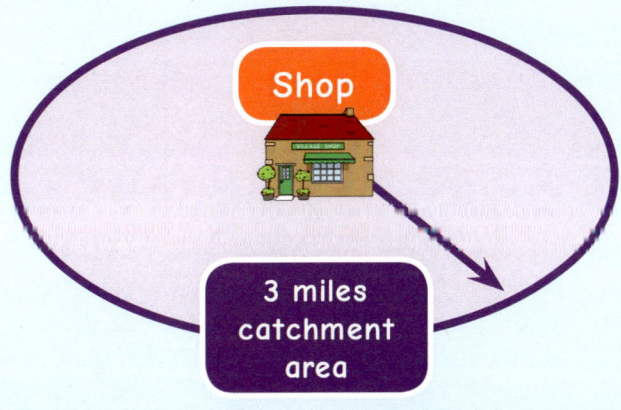

Shop

3 miles catchment area

42 — Low Order Service

- People don't travel far to get **convenience goods**, such as bread and milk.

- Village shops sell convenience goods, where it has a **small range** and is called a **low order service**.

VILLAGE SHOP

Shops and Services

43 Comparison Goods

- For **expensive items**, such as furniture and computers, people **check prices** before buying.
- People **compare** prices, so these are called **comparison goods**.

£150

£360

44 High Order Service

- People will **travel further** to get their sofa or computer.
- So these shops provide a **high order service** and have a **large range**.

SHOP ONLINE FREE UK DELIVERY

National catchment area

45 Public Services

- **Public services** (like libraries, hospitals and schools) also have a **range**.
- You will find a **hospital in a city** as it has a **high threshold** and **high range**.

- You will find a **primary school in a village** with a **low threshold** and a **low range**.

Welcome to St. Michael's Hospital

HOSPITAL

Primary School

High threshold and high range

Low threshold and low range

46 Olympic Athletes Village

- The 2012 London Olympic Athletes Village has been **reused** to become a housing development called **East Village**.

- It has **2,818 houses**.
- They are a mix of private, affordable rental and shared ownership.

47 Where is it?

- It is located within the 27 acres of the Queen Elizabeth Park in London.

48 Facilities in East Village

- It has **30 independent shops** and **cafes**, as well as **health facilities**.

30 independent shops and cafes

This booklet is not to be photocopied. Thank you.

15

Case Study: Olympic Village

49   School Facilities

- There is a **school** for 3 to 18 year olds.
- There are also **playgrounds** for children.

50   Easy To Get To

- London, as well as major airports and shopping centres, are easily **accessible**.

51   Construction Stopped!

- In **May 2011**, construction was stopped while a rare Black Redstart was nesting.

Black Redstart

52   Sustainable Development

- The development in this area is built to be **sustainable**.
- This means it is **improving life without damaging** it for people in years to come.

Sustainable Development

- It does this in a number of ways...

Why is East Village sustainable?

4,000 local jobs were created during construction.

It is well served by public transport. This means less car congestion!

90% of construction waste did **not** go into landfill.

Use of LED lights cuts emissions by 5,000 tonnes per year.

House insulation saves 183,000 tonnes of CO_2 per year.

Only certified timber was used in construction.

Water recycling plant on-site. As a result, one third less water will be used per person than on average in the UK.

Living green roofs planted on all buildings over 100m high. This reduces CO_2 and noise, and encourage wildlife!

Biomass power station on-site provides heat and energy.

53   Urbanisation

- Many people are moving to **urban areas (towns and cities)**.
- This is happening **faster** in **poorer countries**.
- In **richer countries, most** of the **population already live** in urban areas!

I need to move away from here!

54   Poorer Countries

- **Fewer** people in **poorer countries** live in urban areas.
- So today, this means that most **urbanisation** is **happening** in **poorer countries**.

We're all moving!

55   Urbanisation is...

- ...the **growth** of the **number of people** living in **urban areas**.
- It is happening all over the world!
- More than **50%** of the **world's population** live in **urban areas**.
- This increases **daily**.

56   Rural-Urban Migration

- Urbanisation is usually caused by **Rural-Urban migration**.
- This is the **movement of people** from the **countryside to towns** and **cities**.

KS3 Supplement

57   Urbanisation in Poorer Countries

The reasons for moving are <u>different</u> in richer and poorer countries.

People in **poorer countries move** because:

- Of a **shortage** in **services** in **rural areas** (water, healthcare, power).
- If crops fail, farmers may be forced to move to the **city** to **feed their families**.

58   Standard of Living

- People believe that the **standard of living** is better in towns and cities.
- But this **isn't** always the case!
- However, there are usually **more jobs** in urban areas than rural areas.

 **Urbanisation in Developed Countries**

People in **richer countries** move because:

- In the past, **new factories** were built in **urban areas** which created **jobs**.

- **Today**, there is a lot of **redevelopment** in **cities** which makes them more attractive.

 Squatter Settlements

- In poorer countries, **squatter settlements** are a BIG problem (also called **slums** and **shanty towns**).

 Problems of Slums

They are:

- Built **illegally**.
- Built **badly**.
- There is **overcrowding**.
- Built by people who have migrated to the city but **can't afford** proper housing.

I can't afford proper housing...

KS3 Supplement

62   Examples are...

- **Sao Paulo** in Brazil.

- **Mumbai** in India.

63   They can be improved by:

Self-help schemes:
- The government and people **working together.**

64   They can be improved by:

Site and Service:
- People pay a **small rent** for a **site** and can **borrow money** to build or improve their house.
- The rent pays for **services**.

Small rent money

65   They can be improved by:

Local Authority Schemes:
- Funded by the government.
- Offers help to **improve temporary housing** built by residents.

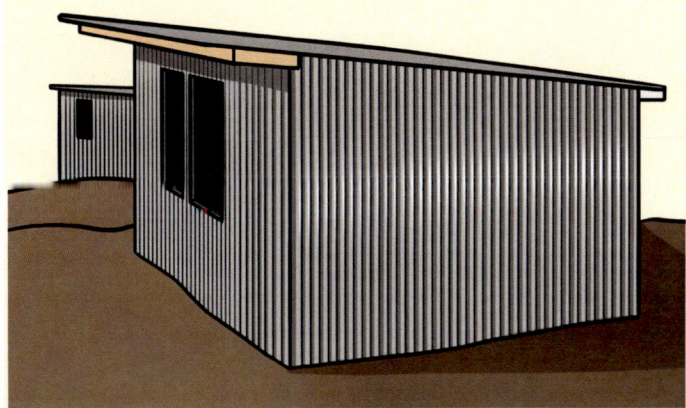

About Oaka Books

Children learn best when they are engaged...

Our aim is to help children enjoy learning by making it fun! That way they will succeed.

This Topic Pack is based on the National Curriculum guidelines for KS3 and ISEB 13+ Common Entrance.

The design and layout of our books follow guidelines from the British Dyslexia Association.

ISBN 978-1-911189-18-3

CE/KS3 Ge-

Settlement

Topic Booklet

9 781911 189183

Three Easy Steps

Read: the easy to follow bullet point Topic Booklet.

Engage: Play the Active Learning Game.

Learn: When you understand the topic, test yourself using the Write Your Own Notes Book. You can use the Topic Booklet to help if you get stuck.

One (short) Topic at a time:

For some students, a big book is a big turn off. That's why we focus on one topic at a time. Short and to the point.

Reading Age

This booklet is suitable for children with a reading age of 10 years 6 months.

Topic Packs for KS1, KS2 & KS3 Include:

History
Geography
Science
French
Maths

Please visit www.oakabooks.co.uk for more information about forthcoming titles.

© Copyright 2018 Oaka Books. All rights reserved.
Written by Kate Doehren, MA Ed, B.Ed Hons, RSA Dip, Sp LD/Dyslexia - Head of Learning Support, Hurstpierpoint College.
Illustrations by Adora Holcroft.

First paperback edition printed 2015 in the United Kingdom.
A catalogue record for this book is available from the British Library.

ISBN 978-1-911189-18-3
No part of this book shall be reproduced or transmitted in any form or by any means, electronic or mechanical, including photocopying, recording or by any information retrieval system without written permission of the copyright owner or a licence permitting restricted copying issued by the Copyright Licensing Agency Ltd, Saffron House, 6-10 Kirby Street, London EC1N 8TS Tel: 020 7400 3100   Fax: 020 7400 3101   Email: cla@cla.co.uk   Web: www.cla.co.uk

Designed, set and published by Oaka™ Books.

To order other titles from Oaka™ Books, please email info@oakabooks.co.uk or visit www.oakabooks.co.uk, or phone: +44 (0) 2392 388519.

Acknowledgements
Our huge thanks go to the many teachers who have been involved in the development of this series of learning guides. Special thanks to Joy Gardiner, for producing hundreds of illustrations, to Kate Doehren, for her enthusiasm and invaluable assistance to my wonderful daughter Sophie, for being the inspiration for the books and, of course, to Charlie, for believing in them.